SONGS OF CHILDHOOD

This edition published 2017
By Living Book Press
147 Durren Rd, Jilliby, 2259
Copyright © Living Book Press, 2017

ISBN: 978-1-925729-09-2

  A catalogue record for this
book is available from the
National Library of Australia

# SONGS OF CHILDHOOD
## WITH SELECTIONS FROM PEACOCK PIE

By
Walter De La Mare

With Illustrations by
Estrella Canziani

LIVING BOOK PRESS

2017

# Contents - Songs of Childhood

| | | | | |
|---|---|---|---|---|
| Sleepyhead | 1 | | Haunted | 77 |
| O Dear Me! | 3 | | The Sleeping Beauty | 78 |
| Bluebells | 5 | | The Supper | 79 |
| Lovelocks | 6 | | The Horn | 81 |
| A-Tishooo | 7 | | Captain Lean | 82 |
| Tartary | 8 | | The Portrait of a Warrior | 83 |
| The Buckle | 12 | | The Isle of Lone | 84 |
| The Hare | 13 | | The Ravens Tomb | 94 |
| Bunches of Grapes | 14 | | The Christening | 95 |
| John Mouldy | 15 | | The Funeral | 97 |
| The Fly | 16 | | The Mother Bird | 98 |
| Song | 17 | | The Child In The Story Goes To Bed | 99 |
| I saw Three Witches | 19 | | The Child In The Story Awakes | 102 |
| The Silver Penny | 20 | | Cecil | 104 |
| The Rainbow | 21 | | The Lamplighter | 107 |
| The Night-Swans | 22 | | I Met At Eve | 108 |
| Reverie | 24 | | Lullaby | 110 |
| The Three Beggars | 27 | | Envoy | 112 |
| Alulvan | 29 | | | |
| The Pedlar | 31 | | | |
| The Grey Wolf | 34 | | | |
| Dame Hickory | 35 | | | |
| The Fairies Dancing | 37 | | | |
| The Miller and His Son | 38 | | | |
| The Ogre | 41 | | | |
| The Gage | 44 | | | |
| The Dwarf | 49 | | | |
| The Pilgrim | 53 | | | |
| The Fiddlers | 57 | | | |
| As Lucy Went A-Walking | 59 | | | |
| Down-Adown-Derry | 63 | | | |
| The Englishman | 67 | | | |
| The Phantom | 71 | | | |

# Contents - From Peacock Pie

## UP AND DOWN

| | |
|---|---|
| The Horseman | 113 |
| Up and Down | 113 |
| Mrs. Earth | 114 |
| Alas, Alack | 114 |
| Tired Time | 115 |
| Mima | 115 |
| The Huntsmen | 116 |
| The Bandog | 116 |
| I Can't Abear | 117 |
| The Dunce | 117 |
| Chicken | 118 |
| Some One | 118 |
| Bread and Cherries | 119 |
| Old Shellover | 119 |
| Hapless | 120 |
| The Little Bird | 120 |
| Cake and Sack | 121 |
| The Ship of Rio | 122 |
| Tillie | 123 |
| Jim Jay | 124 |
| Miss T. | 125 |
| The Cupboard | 126 |
| The Barber's | 127 |
| Hide and Seek | 128 |

## BOYS AND GIRLS

| | |
|---|---|
| Then | 129 |
| The Window | 129 |
| Poor Henry | 130 |
| Full Moon | 130 |
| The Bookworm | 131 |
| The Quartette | 132 |
| Mistletoe | 133 |
| The Lost Shoe | 134 |
| The Truants | 135 |

## SLEEPYHEAD

As I lay awake in the white moonlight,
I heard a sweet singing in the wood—
   'Out of bed,
   Sleepyhead,
Put your white foot now,
   Here are we,
   'Neath the tree,
Singing round the root now!'


I looked out of window in the white moonlight,
The trees were like snow in the wood—
   'Come away
   Child and play,
Light with the gnomies;
   In a mound,
   Green and round—
That's where their home is!
   'Honey-sweet,
   Curds to eat,
Cream and frumenty,
   Shells and beads,
   Poppy seeds,
You shall have plenty.'

But soon as I stooped in the dim moonlight
To put on my stocking and my shoe,
The sweet, sweet singing died sadly away,
And the light of the morning peeped through:
Then instead of the gnomies there came a red robin
To sing of the buttercups and dew.

## O DEAR ME!

Here are crocuses, white, gold, grey!
    'O dear me!' says Marjorie May;
Flat as a platter the blackberry blows:
    'O dear me!' says Madeleine Rose;
The leaves are fallen, the swallows flown:
    'O dear me!' says Humphrey John;
Snow lies thick where all night it fell:
    'O dear me!' says Emmanuel.

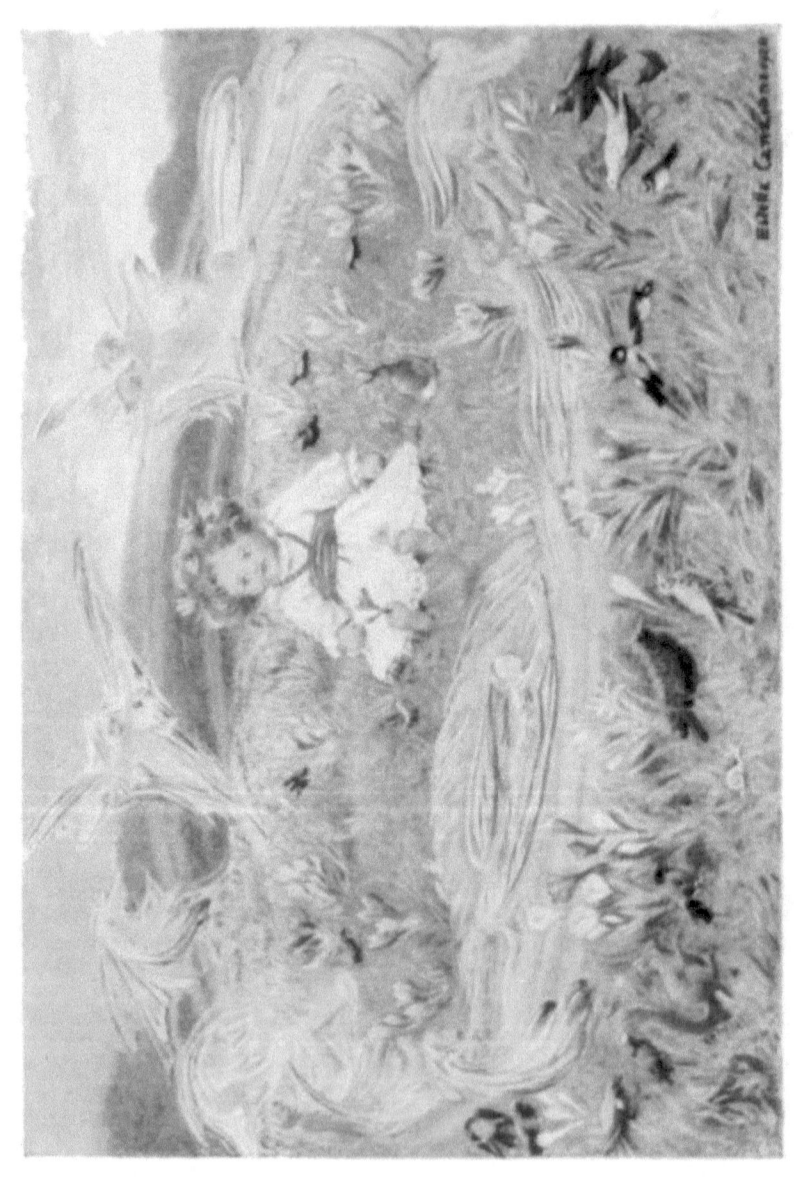

## BLUEBELLS

Where the bluebells and the wind are,
    Fairies in a ring I spied,
And I heard a little linnet
Singing near beside.

Where the primrose and the dew are,
Soon were sped the fairies all:
Only now the green turf freshens,
And the linnets call.

## LOVELOCKS

I watched the Lady Caroline
Bind up her dark and beauteous hair;
Her face was rosy in the glass,
And 'twixt the coils her hands would pass,
    White in the candleshine.

Her bottles on the table lay,
Stoppered yet sweet of violet;
Her image in the mirror stooped
To view those locks as lightly looped
    As cherry-boughs in May.

The snowy night lay dim without,
I heard the Waits their sweet song sing;
The window smouldered keen with frost;
Yet still she twisted, sleeked and tossed
    Her beauteous hair about.

## A-TISHOO

Sneeze, Pretty, Sneeze, Dainty,
Else the Elves will have you sure;
Sneeze, Light-of-Seven-Bright-Candles,
See they're tipping at the door;
Their wee feet in measure falling,
All their little voices calling—
Sneeze, or never come no more!'
      'A-Tishoo!'

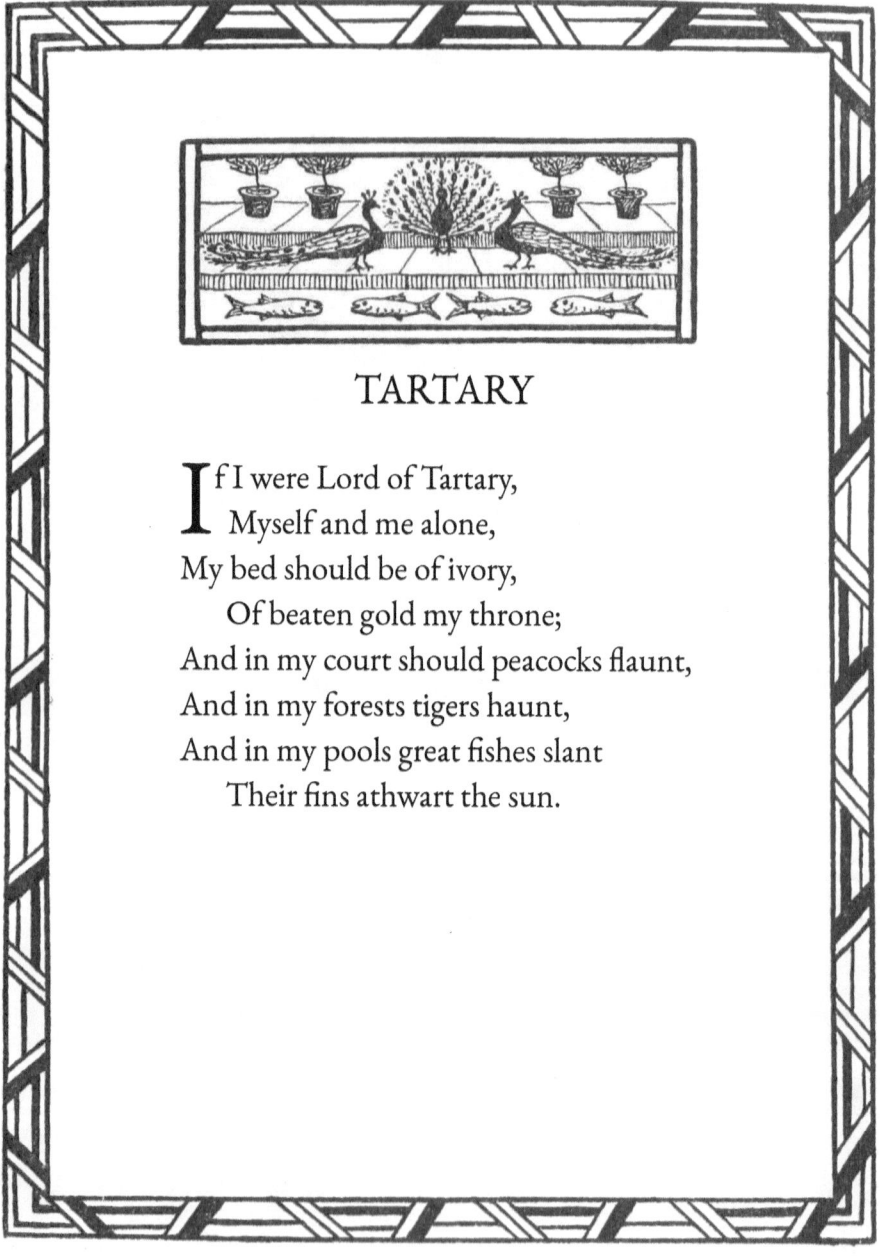

# TARTARY

If I were Lord of Tartary,
   Myself and me alone,
My bed should be of ivory,
   Of beaten gold my throne;
And in my court should peacocks flaunt,
And in my forests tigers haunt,
And in my pools great fishes slant
   Their fins athwart the sun.

If I were Lord of Tartary,
    Trumpeters every day
To all my meals should summon me,
    And in my courtyards bray;
And in the evenings lamps should shine,
Yellow as honey, red as wine,
While harp, and flute, and mandoline,
    Made music sweet and gay.

If I were Lord of Tartary,
    I'd wear a robe of beads,
White, and gold, and green they'd be—
    And small, and thick as seeds;
And ere should wane the morning-star,
I'd don my robe and scimitar,
And zebras seven should draw my car
    Through Tartary's dark glades.

Lord of the fruits of Tartary,
    Her rivers silver-pale!
Lord of the hills of Tartary,
    Glen, thicket, wood, and dale!
Her flashing stars, her scented breeze,
Her trembling lakes, like foamless seas,
Her bird-delighting citron-trees
    In every purple vale!

## THE BUCKLE

I had a silver buckle,
I sewed it on my shoe,
And 'neath a sprig of mistletoe
I danced the evening through!

I had a bunch of cowslips,
I hid 'em in a grot,
In case the elves should come by night
And me remember not.

I had a yellow riband,
I tied it in my hair,
That, walking in the garden,
The birds might see it there.

I had a secret laughter,
I laughed it near the wall:
Only the ivy and the wind
May tell of it at all.

# THE HARE

In the black furrow of a field
I saw an old witch-hare this night;
And she cocked her lissome ear,
And she eyed the moon so bright,
And she nibbled o' the green;
And I whispered 'Whsst! witch-hare,'
Away like a ghostie o'er the field
She fled, and left the moonlight there.

## BUNCHES OF GRAPES

'Bunches of grapes,' says Timothy;
'Pomegranates pink,' says Elaine;
'A junket of cream and a cranberry tart
    For me,' says Jane.

'Love-in-a-mist,' says Timothy;
'Primroses pale,' says Elaine;
'A nosegay of pinks and mignonette
    For me,' says Jane.

'Chariots of gold,' says Timothy;
'Silvery wings,' says Elaine;
'A bumpity ride in a wagon of hay
    For me,' says Jane.

# JOHN MOULDY

I spied John Mouldy in his cellar,
Deep down twenty steps of stone;
In the dusk he sat a-smiling,
    Smiling there alone.

He read no book, he snuffed no candle;
The rats ran in, the rats ran out;
And far and near, the drip of water
    Went whisp'ring about.

The dusk was still, with dew a-falling,
I saw the Dog-star bleak and grim,
I saw a slim brown rat of Norway
    Creep over him.

I spied John Mouldy in his cellar,
Deep down twenty steps of stone;
In the dusk he sat a-smiling,
    Smiling there alone.

# THE FLY

How large unto the tiny fly
    Must little things appear!—
A rosebud like a feather bed,
    Its prickle like a spear;

A dewdrop like a looking-glass,
    A hair like golden wire;
The smallest grain of mustard-seed
    As fierce as coals of fire;

A loaf of bread, a lofty hill;
    A wasp, a cruel leopard;
And specks of salt as bright to see
    As lambkins to a shepherd.

# SONG

O for a moon to light me home!
    O for a lanthorn green!
For those sweet stars the Pleiades,
That glitter in the twilight trees;
    O for a lovelorn taper! O
    For a lanthorn green!

O for a frock of tartan!
    O for clear, wild, grey eyes!
For fingers light as violets,
'Neath branches that the blackbird frets;
    O for a thistly meadow! O
    For clear, wild grey eyes!

O for a heart like almond boughs!
    O for sweet thoughts like rain!
O for first-love like fields of grey,
Shut April-buds at break of day!
    O for a sleep like music!
    For still dreams like rain!

## I SAW THREE WITCHES

I saw three witches
That bowed down like barley,
And took to their brooms 'neath a louring sky,
And, mounting a storm-cloud,
Aloft on its margin,
Stood black in the silver as up they did fly.

I saw three witches
That mocked the poor sparrows
They carried in cages of wicker along,
Till a hawk from his eyrie
Swooped down like an arrow,
Smote on the cages, and ended their song.

I saw three witches
That sailed in a shallop,
All turning their heads with a truculent smile,
Till a bank of green osiers
Concealed their grim faces,
Though I heard them lamenting for many a mile.

I saw three witches
Asleep in a valley,
Their heads in a row, like stones in a flood,
Till the moon, creeping upward,
Looked white through the valley,
And turned them to bushes in bright scarlet bud.

## THE SILVER PENNY

'Sailorman, I'll give to you
    My bright silver penny,
If out to sea you'll sail me
    And my dear sister Jenny.'

'Get in, young sir, I'll sail ye
    And your dear sister Jenny,
But pay she shall her golden locks
    Instead of your penny.'

They sail away, they sail away,
    O fierce the winds blew!
The foam flew in clouds,
    And dark the night grew!

And all the wild sea-water
    Climbed steep into the boat;
Back to the shore again
    Sail they will not.

Drowned is the sailorman,
    Drowned is sweet Jenny,
And drowned in the deep sea
    A bright silver penny.

## THE RAINBOW

I saw the lovely arch
Of Rainbow span the sky,
The gold sun burning
As the rain swept by.

In bright-tinged solitude
The showery foliage shone
One lovely moment--
And the Bow was gone

## THE NIGHT-SWANS

'Tis silence on the enchanted lake,
   And silence in the air serene,
Save for the beating of her heart,
   The lovely-eyed Evangeline.

She sings across the waters clear
   And dark with trees and stars between,
The notes her fairy godmother
   Taught her, the child Evangeline.

As might the unrippled pool reply,
   Faltering an answer far and sweet,
Three swans as white as mountain snow
   Swim mantling to her feet.

And still upon the lake they stay,
   Their eyes black stars in all their snow,
And softly, in the glassy pool,
   Their feet beat darkly to and fro.

She rides upon her little boat,
Her swans swim through the starry sheen,
Rowing her into Fairyland—
The lovely-eyed Evangeline.

'Tis silence on the enchanted lake,
And silence in the air serene;
Voices shall call in vain again
On earth the child Evangeline.

'Evangeline! Evangeline!'
Upstairs, downstairs, all in vain.
Her room is dim; her flowers faded;
She answers not again.

## REVERIE

When slim Sophia mounts her horse
    And paces down the avenue,
It seems an inward melody
    She paces to.

Each narrow hoof is lifted high
    Beneath the dark enclust'ring pines,
A silver ray within his bit
    And bridle shines.

His eye burns deep, his tail is arched,
    And streams upon the shadowy air,
The daylight sleeks his jetty flanks,
    His mistress' hair.

Her habit flows in darkness down,
    Upon the stirrup rests her foot,
Her brow is lifted, as if earth
    She heeded not.

'Tis silent in the avenue,
    The sombre pines are mute of song,
The blue is dark, there moves no breeze
    The boughs among.

When slim Sophia mounts her horse
    And paces down the avenue,
It seems an inward melody
    She paces to.

## THE THREE BEGGARS

Twas autumn daybreak gold and wild,
    While past St Ann's grey tower they shuffled,
Three beggars spied a fairy-child
    In crimson mantle muffled.

The daybreak lighted up her face
    All pink, and sharp, and emerald-eyed;
She looked on them a little space,
    And shrill as hautboy cried:—

'O three tall footsore men of rags
    Which walking this gold morn I see,
What will ye give me from your bags
    For fairy kisses three?'

The first, that was a reddish man,
    Out of his bundle takes a crust:
'La, by the tombstones of St Ann,
    There's fee, if fee ye must!'

The second, that was a chesnut man,
    Out of his bundle draws a bone:
'La, by the belfry of St Ann,
    And all my breakfast gone!'

The third, that was a yellow man,
    Out of his bundle picks a groat,
'La, by the Angel of St Ann,
        And I must go without.'

That changeling, lean and icy-lipped,
    Touched crust, and bone, and groat, and lo!
Beneath her finger taper-tipped
        The magic all ran through.

Instead of crust a peacock pie,
    Instead of bone sweet venison,
Instead of groat a white lilie
        With seven blooms thereon.

And each fair cup was deep with wine:
    Such was the changeling's charity,
The sweet feast was enough for nine,
        But not too much for three.

O toothsome meat in jelly froze!
    O tender haunch of elfin stag!
O rich the odour that arose!
        O plump with scraps each bag!

There, in the daybreak gold and wild,
    Each merry-hearted beggar man
Drank deep unto the fairy child,
        And blessed the good St Ann.

## ALULVAN

The sun is clear of bird and cloud,
　The grass shines windless, grey, and still,
In dusky ruin the owl dreams on,
The cuckoo echoes on the hill;
　　Yet soft along Alulvan's walks
　　　　The ghost at noonday stalks.

His eyes in shadow of his hat
Stare on the ruins of his house;
His cloak, up-fasten'd with a brooch,
Of faded velvet grey as mouse,
　　Brushes the roses as he goes:
　　　　Yet wavers not one rose.

The wild birds in a cloud fly up
From their sweet feeding in the fruit;
The droning of the bees and flies
Rises gradual as a lute;
　　Is it for fear the birds are flown,
　　　　And shrills the insect-drone?

Thick is the ivy o'er Alulvan,
And crisp with summer-heat its turf;
Far, far across its empty pastures
Alulvan's sands are white with surf:
    And he himself is grey as sea,
        Watching beneath an elder-tree.

All night the fretful, shrill Banshee
Lurks in the chambers' dark festoons,
Calling for ever, o'er garden and river,
Through magpie changing of the moons:
    'Alulvan, O, alas! Alulvan,
        The doom of lone Alulvan!'

# THE PEDLAR

There came a Pedlar to an evening house;
   Sweet Lettice, from her lattice looking down,
Wondered what man he was, so curious
His black hair dangled on his tattered gown:
Then lifts he up his face, with glittering eyes,—
'What will you buy, sweetheart?—Here's honeycomb,
And mottled pippins, and sweet mulberry pies,
Comfits and peaches, snowy cherry bloom,
To keep in water for to make night sweet:
All that you want, sweetheart,—come, taste and eat!'

Ev'n with his sugared words, returned to her
The clear remembrance of a gentle voice:—
'And O! my child, should ever a flatterer
Tap with his wares, and promise of all joys
And vain sweet pleasures that on earth may be;
Seal up your ears, sing some old happy song,
Confuse his magic who is all mockery:
His sweets are death.' Yet, still, how she doth long
But just to taste, then shut the lattice tight,
And hide her eyes from the delicious sight!

'What must I pay?' she whispered. 'Pay!' says he,
'Pedlar I am who through this wood do roam,
One lock of hair is gold enough for me,
For apple, peach, comfit, or honeycomb!'
But from her bough a drowsy squirrel cried,
'Trust him not, Lettice, trust, oh trust him not!'
And many another woodland tongue beside
Rose softly in the silence—'Trust him not!'
Then cried the Pedlar in a bitter voice,
'What, in the thicket, is this idle noise?'

A late, harsh blackbird smote him with her wings,
As through the glade, dark in the dim, she flew;
Yet still the Pedlar his old burden sings,—
'What, pretty sweetheart, shall I show to you?
Here's orange ribands, here's a string of pearls,
Here's silk of buttercup and pansy glove,
A pin of tortoiseshell for windy curls,
A box of silver, scented sweet with clove:
Come now,' he says, with dim and lifted face,
'I pass not often such a lonely place.'

'Pluck not a hair!' a hidden rabbit cried,
'With but one hair he'll steal thy heart away,
Then only sorrow shall thy lattice hide:
Go in! all honest pedlars come by day.'
There was dead silence in the drowsy wood;
'Here's syrup for to lull sweet maids to sleep;

And bells for dreams, and fairy wine and food
All day thy heart in happiness to keep';—
And now she takes the scissors on her thumb,—
'O, then, no more unto my lattice come!'

O sad the sound of weeping in the wood!
Now only night is where the Pedlar was;
And bleak as frost upon a too-sweet bud
His magic steals in darkness, O alas!
Why all the summer doth sweet Lettice pine?
And, ere the wheat is ripe, why lies her gold
Hid 'neath fresh new-pluckt sprigs of eglantine?
Why all the morning hath the cuckoo tolled,
Sad to and fro in green and secret ways,
With lonely bells the burden of his days?

And, in the market-place, what man is this
Who wears a loop of gold upon his breast,
Stuck heartwise; and whose glassy flatteries
Take all the townsfolk ere they go to rest
Who come to buy and gossip? Doth his eye
Remember a face lovely in a wood?
O people! hasten, hasten, do not buy
His woful wares; the bird of grief doth brood
There where his heart should be; and far away
Dew lies on grave-flowers this selfsame day!

## THE GREY WOLF

'A fagot, a fagot, go fetch for the fire, son!'
    'O, Mother, the wolf looks in at the door!'
'Cry Shoo! now, cry Shoo! thou fierce grey wolf
        fly, now;
    Haste thee away, he will fright thee no more.'

'I ran, O, I ran, but the grey wolf ran faster,
    O, Mother, I cry in the air at thy door,
Cry Shoo! now, cry Shoo! but his fangs
        were so cruel,
    Thy son (save his hatchet) thou'lt never
        see more.'

# DAME HICKORY

'Dame Hickory, Dame Hickory,
　　Here's sticks for your fire,
Furze-twigs, and oak-twigs,
　　And beech-twigs, and briar!'
But when old Dame Hickory came for to see,
She found 'twas the voice of the false faerie.

'Dame Hickory, Dame Hickory,
　　Here's meat for your broth,
Goose-flesh, and hare's flesh,
　　And pig's trotters both!'
But when old Dame Hickory came for to see,
She found 'twas the voice of the false faerie.

'Dame Hickory, Dame Hickory,
　　Here's a wolf at your door,
His teeth grinning white,
　　And his tongue wagging sore!'
'Nay!' said Dame Hickory, 'ye false faerie!'
But a wolf 'twas indeed, and famished was he.

'Dame Hickory, Dame Hickory,
　　Here's buds for your tomb,
Bramble, and lavender,
　　And rosemary bloom!'
'Hush!' said Dame Hickory, 'ye false faerie,
Ye cry like a wolf, ye do, and trouble poor me.'

## THE FAIRIES DANCING

I heard along the early hills,
  Ere yet the lark was risen up,
Ere yet the dawn with firelight fills
The night-dew of the bramble-cup,—
I heard the fairies in a ring
Sing as they tripped a lilting round
Soft as the moon on wavering wing.
The starlight shook as if with sound,
As if with echoing, and the stars
Prankt their bright eyes with trembling gleams;
While red with war the gusty Mars
Rained upon earth his ruddy beams.
He shone alone, adown the West,
While I, behind a hawthorn-bush,
Watched on the fairies flaxen-tressed
The fires of the morning flush.
Till, as a mist, their beauty died,
Their singing shrill and fainter grew;
And daylight tremulous and wide
Flooded the moorland through and through;
Till Urdon's copper weathercock
Was reared in golden flame afar,
And dim from moonlit dreams awoke
The towers and groves of Arroar.

## THE MILLER AND HIS SON

A twangling harp for Mary,
    A silvery flute for John,
And now we'll play the livelong day,
    'The Miller and his Son.'

'The Miller went a-walking
    All in the forest high,
He sees three doves a-flitting
    Against the dark blue sky:

'Says he, "My son, now follow
    These doves so white and free,
That cry above the forest,
    And surely cry to thee."

"I go, my dearest Father,
    But O! I sadly fear,
These doves so white will lead me far,
    But never bring me near."

'He kisses the Miller,
    He cries, "Awhoop to ye!"
And straightway through the forest
    Follows the wood-doves three.

'There came a sound of weeping
    To the Miller in his Mill;
Red roses in a thicket
    Bloomed over near his wheel;

'Three stars shone wild and brightly
  Above the forest dim:
But never his dearest son
  Returns again to him.

'The cuckoo shall call "Cuckoo!"
  In vain along the vale,
The linnet, and the blackbird,
  The mournful nightingale;

'The Miller hears and sees not,
  A-thinking of his son;
His toppling wheel is silent;
  His grinding done.

'"Ye doves so white," he weepeth,
  "Ye roses on the tree,
Ye stars that shine so brightly,
  Ye shine in vain for me!"

'I bade him follow, follow,
  He said, "O Father dear,
These doves so white will lead me far
  But never bring me near!"'

A twangling harp for Mary,
  A silvery flute for John,
And now we'll play the livelong day,
  'The Miller and his Son.'

# THE OGRE

'Tis moonlight on Trebarwith Vale,
    And moonlight on an Ogre keen,
Who prowling hungry through the dale
    A lone cottage hath seen.

Small with thin smoke ascending up
    Three casements and a door:—
The Ogre eager is to sup,
    And here seems dainty store.

Sweet as a larder to a mouse,
    So to him staring down,
Seemed the sweet-windowed moonlit house,
    With jasmine overgrown.

He snorted, as the billows snort
    In darkness of the night,
Betwixt his lean locks tawny-swart,
    He glowered on the sight.

Into the garden sweet with peas
    He put his wooden shoe,
And bending back the apple trees
    Crept covetously through;

Then, stooping, with an impious eye
    Stared through the lattice small,
And spied two children which did lie
    Asleep, against the wall.

Into their dreams no shadow fell,
    Of his disastrous thumb
Groping discreet, and gradual,
    Across the quiet room.

But scarce his nail had scraped the cot
    Wherein these children lay,
As if his malice were forgot,
    It suddenly did stay.

For faintly in the ingle-nook
    He heard a cradlesong,
That rose into his thoughts and woke
    Terror them among.

For she who in the kitchen sat
    Darning by the fire,
Guileless of what he would be at,
    Sang sweet as wind or wire:—

'Lullay, thou little tiny child,
    By-by, lullay, lullie;
Jesu of glory, meek and mild,
    This night remember ye!

'Fiend, witch, and goblin, foul and wild,
    He deems 'em smoke to be;
Lullay, thou little tiny child,
    By-by, lullay, lullie!'

The Ogre lifted up his eyes
    Into the moon's pale ray,
And gazed upon her leopard-wise,
    Cruel and clear as day;

He snarled in gluttony and fear:
    'The wind blows dismally,
Jesu in storm my lambs be near,
    By-by, lullay, lullie!'

And like a ravenous beast which sees
    The hunter's icy eye,
So did this wretch in wrath confess
    Sweet Jesu's mastery.

He lightly drew his greedy thumb
    From out that casement pale,
And strode, enormous, swiftly home,
    Whinnying down the dale.

## THE GAGE

Lady Jane, O Lady Jane!
Your hound hath broken bounds again,
  And chased my timorous deer, O;
    If him I see,
    That hour he'll dee;
My brakes shall be his bier, O.'

'Hoots! lord, speak not so proud to me!
My hound, I trow, is fleet and free,
  He's welcome to your deer, O;
    Shoot, shoot you may,
    He'll gang his way,
Your threats we nothing fear, O.'

He's fetched him in, he's fetched him in,
Gone all his swiftness, all his din,
  White fang, and glowering eye, O:
    'Here is your beast,
    And now at least
My herds in peace shall lie, O.'

"In peace!" my lord, O mark me well!
For what my jolly hound befell
  You shall sup twenty-fold, O!
    For every tooth
    Of his, i'sooth,
A stag in pawn I hold, O.

'Huntsman and horn, huntsman and horn,
Shall scare your heaths and coverts lorn,
    Braying 'em shrill and clear, O;
    But lone and still
        Shall lift each hill,
Each valley wan and sere, O.

'Ride up you may, ride down you may,
Lonely or trooped, by night or day,
    My hound shall haunt you ever:
        Bird, beast, and game
        Shall dread the same,
The wild fish of your river.'

Her cheek is like the angry rose,
Her eye with wrath and pity flows:
    He gazes fierce and round, O,—
        'Dear Lord!' he says,
        'What loveliness
To waste upon a hound, O.

'I'd give my stags, my hills and dales,
My stormcocks and my nightingales
    To have undone this deed, O;
        For deep beneath
        My heart is death
Which for her love doth bleed, O.'

Wanders he up, wanders he down,
On foot, a-horse, by night and noon:
    His lands are bleak and drear, O;
        Forsook his dales
        Of nightingales,
Forsook his moors of deer, O.

Forsook his heart, ah me! of mirth;
There's nothing lightsome left on earth:
    Only one scene is fain, O,
      Where far remote
      The moonbeams gloat,
And sleeps the lovely Jane, O.

Until an eve when lone he went,
Gnawing his beard in dreariment,
    Lo! from a thicket hidden,
        Lovely as flower
        In April hour,
Steps forth a form unbidden.

'Get ye now down, Lord Aërie,
I'm troubled so I'm like to dee,'
    She cries, 'twixt joy and grief, O;
        'The hound is dead,
        When all is said,
But love is past belief, O.

'Nights, nights I've lain your lands to see,
Forlorn and still—and all for me,
    All for a foolish curse, O;
        Now here am I
        Come out to die,
To live unlov'd is worse, O!'

In faith, this lord, in that lone dale,
Hears now a sweeter nightingale,
    And lairs a tend'rer deer, O;
        His sorrow goes
        Like mountain snows
In waters sweet and clear, O!

Let the hound bay in Shadowland,
Tuning his ear to understand
    What voice hath tamed this Aërie;
        Chafe, chafe he may
        The stag all day,
And never thirst nor weary.

Now here he smells, now there he smells,
Winding his voice along the dells,
    Till grey flows up the morn, O;
        Then hies again
        To Lady Jane,
No longer now forlorn, O.

Ay, as it were a bud, did break
To loveliness for Aërie's sake,
    So she in beauty moving
        Rides at his hand
        Across his land,
Beloved as well as loving.

# THE DWARF

Now, Jinnie, my dear, to the dwarf be off,
  That lives in Barberry Wood,
And fetch me some honey, but be sure you don't laugh,—
  He hates little girls that are rude, are rude,
    He hates little girls that are rude.'

Jane tapped at the door of the house in the wood,
  And the dwarf looked over the wall,
He eyed her so queer, 'twas as much as she could
  To keep from laughing at all, at all,
    To keep from laughing at all.

His shoes down the passage came clod, clod, clod,
  And when he opened the door,
He croaked so harsh, 'twas as much as she could
  To keep from laughing the more, the more,
    To keep from laughing the more.

As there, with his bushy red beard, he stood,
  Pricked out to double its size,
He squinted so cross, 'twas as much as she could
  To keep the tears out of her eyes, her eyes,
    To keep the tears out of her eyes.

He slammed the door, and went clod, clod, clod,
    But while in the porch she bides,
He squealed so fierce, 'twas as much as she could
    To keep from cracking her sides, her sides,
    To keep from cracking her sides.

He threw a pumpkin over the wall,
    And melons and apples beside,
So thick in the air, that to see 'em all fall,
    She laughed, and laughed, till she cried, cried, cried,
    Jane laughed and laughed till she cried.

Down fell her teardrops a pit-apat-pat,
    And red as a rose she grew;—
'Kah! kah!' said the dwarf, 'is it crying you're at?
    It's the very worst thing you could do, do, do,
    It's the very worst thing you could do.'

He slipped like a monkey up into a tree,
    He shook her down cherries like rain;
'See now,' says he, cheeping, 'a blackbird I be,
    Laugh, laugh, little Jinnie, again-gain-gain,
    Laugh, laugh, little Jinnie, again.'

Ah me! what a strange, what a gladsome duet
    From a house i' the deeps of a wood!
Such shrill and such harsh voices never met yet
    A-laughing as loud as they could-could-could,

A-laughing as loud as they could.
Come Jinnie, come dwarf, cocksparrow, and bee,
　　There's a ring gaudy-green in the dell,
Sing, sing, ye sweet cherubs, that flit in the tree;
　　La! who can draw tears from a well-well-well,
　　　Who ever drew tears from a well!

# THE PILGRIM

'Shall we carry now your bundle,
  You old grey man?
Over hill and over meadow,
Lighter than an owlet's shadow,
We will whirl it through the air,
Through blue regions shrill and bare;
Shall we carry now your bundle,
      You old grey man?'

The Pilgrim lifted up his eyes
And saw three fiends, in the skies,
Stooping o'er that lonely place
      Evil in form and face.

'Nay,' he answered, 'leave me, leave me—
      Ye three wild fiends!
Far it is my feet must wander;
And my city lieth yonder;
I must bear my bundle alone,
      Till the day be done.'

The fiends stared down with leaden eye,
Fanning the chill air duskily,
'Twixt their hoods they stoop and cry:—
'Shall we smooth the path before you,
      You old grey man?

Sprinkle it green with gilded showers,
Strew it o'er with painted flowers?
Shall we blow sweet airs on it,
Lure bright birds to sing and flit?
Shall we smooth the path before you,
    You old grey man?'

'O 'tis better silence, silence!
    Ye three wild fiends!
I am footsore, faint and weary—
Dark the way, forlorn and dreary—
Beaten of wind, torn of briar,
Smitten of rain, parched with fire—
But 'tis better silence,
    Ye three wild fiends!'

It seemed a cloud obscured the air,
Lightning quivered in the gloom,
And a faint voice of thunder spake
Far in the lone hill-hollows—'Come!'
Then, half in fury, half in dread,
The fiends drew closer down and said:

'Nay, thou foolish fond old man,
      Hearken awhile!
Frozen, scorched, with ice and heat!
Tarry now, sit down and eat;
Juice of purple grape shall be
Youth and solace unto thee.

Music of tambour, wire and wind,
Ease shall bring to heart and mind;
Wonderrful sweet mouths shall sigh
Languishing and lullaby;
Rest, then, lest this night you die,
      Stubborn old man.'

The pilgrim crouches terrified
At stooping hood, and glassy face,
Gloating, evil, side by side;
Terror and hate brood o'er the place;
He flings his withered hands on high
With a bitter, breaking cry:—
'Pity have, and leave me, leave me,
      Ye three wild fiends:

If I lay me down in slumber,
Then I lay me down in wrath;
If I stir not in sweet dreaming,
Then I wither in my path;
If I hear sweet voices singing,
'Tis a demon's lullaby;
And in "hideous storm and terror"
    I wake but to die!'

And even while he spake, on high
Arrows of sunlight pierced the sky.
Bright streamed the rain. O'er buring snow
From hill to hill a wondrous bow
Of colour and fire trembled in air,
Painting its heavenly beauty there.

Wild flapped each fiend a batlike hood
'Gainst that affrighting light, and stood
Bearing the windless rain, and then
Rose heavey and slow with cowering head,
Circled in company again,
And into darkness fled.
Marvellous sweet it was to hear
The waters gushing loud and clear;
Marvellous happy it was to be
Alone, and yet not solitary;
Oh, out of terror and dark to come
    In sight of home!

## THE FIDDLERS

Nine feat Fiddlers had good Queen Bess
To play her music as she did dress.
Behind an arras of horse and hound
They sate there scraping delightsome sound.
Spangled, bejewelled, her skirts would she
Draw o'er a petticoat of cramasie;
And soft each string like a bird would sing
In the starry dusk of evening.
Then slow from the deeps the crisscross bows,
Crooning like doves, arose and arose.
And when, like a cage, her ladies did raise
A stiff rich splendour o'er her ribbed stays,
Like bumbling bees those four times nine
Fingers in melodies loud did pine;
Till came her coif and her violet shoon
And her virgin face shone out like the moon:
Oh, then in a rapture those three times three
Fiddlers squealed shrill on their topmost C.

## AS LUCY WENT A-WALKING

As Lucy went a-walking one wintry morning fine,
There sate three crows upon a bough, and three times three is nine:
Then 'O!' said Lucy, in the snow, 'it's very plain to see
A witch has been a-walking in the fields in front of me.'

Then stept she light and heedfully across the frozen snow,
And plucked a bunch of elder-twigs that near a pool did grow:
And, by and by, she comes to seven shadows in one place
Stretched by seven poplar-trees against the sun's bright face.

She looks to left, she looks to right, and in the midst she sees
A little well of water clear and frozen 'neath the trees;
Then down beside its margent in the crusty snow she kneels,
And hears a magic belfry a-ringing with sweet bells.

But when the belfry ceased to sound yet nothing could she see,
Save only frozen water in the shadow of the tree.
But presently she lifted up her eyes along the snow,
And sees a witch in brindled shawl a-frisking to and fro.

Her shoes were buckled scarlet that capered to and fro,
And all her rusty locks were wreathed with twisted mistletoe;
But never a dint, or mark, or print, in the whiteness for to see,
Though danced she high, though danced she fast, though danced she lissomely.

It seemed 'twas diamonds in the air, or little flakes of frost;
It seemed 'twas golden smoke around, or sunbeams lightly tost;
It seemed an elfin music like to reeds and warblers rose:
'Nay!' Lucy said, 'it is the wind that through the branches flows.'

And as she peeps, and as she peeps, 'tis no more one, but three,
And eye of bat, and downy wing of owl within the tree,
And the bells of that sweet belfry a-pealing as before,
And now it is not three she sees, and now it is not four.

'O! who are ye,' sweet Lucy cries, 'that in a dreadful ring,
All muffled up in brindled shawls, do caper, frisk, and spring?'
'A witch and witches, one and nine,' they straight to her reply,
And looked upon her narrowly, with green and needle eye.

Then Lucy sees in clouds of gold sweet cherry-trees upgrow,
And bushes of red roses that bloomed above the snow;
She smells all faint the almond-boughs that blow so wild and fair,
And doves with milky eyes ascend fluttering in the air.

Clear flowers she sees, like tulip buds, go floating by like birds,
With wavering tips that warbled sweetly strange enchanted words;
And as with ropes of amethyst the boughs with lamps were hung,
And clusters of green emeralds like fruit upon them clung.

'O witches nine, ye dreadful nine, O witches seven and three!
Whence come these wondrous things that I this Christmas
        morning see?'
But straight, as in a clap, when she of Christmas says the word,
Here is the snow, and there the sun, but never bloom nor bird;

Nor warbling flame, nor gloaming-rope of amethyst there shows,
Nor bunches of green emeralds, nor belfry, well, and rose,
Nor cloud of gold, nor cherry-tree, nor witch in brindled shawl,
But like a dream which vanishes, so vanished were they all.

When Lucy sees, and only sees, three crows upon a bough,
And earthly twigs, and bushes hidden white in driven snow,
Then 'O!' said Lucy, 'three times three is nine—I plainly see
Some witch has been a-walking in the fields in front of me.'

## DOWN-ADOWN-DERRY

Down-adown-derry,
Sweet Annie Maroon,
Gathering daisies
In the meadows of Doone,
Hears a shrill piping,
Elflike and free,
Where the waters go brawling
In rills to the sea;
    Singing down-adown-derry.

Down-adown-derry,
Sweet Annie Maroon,
Through the green grasses
Peeps softly; and soon
Spies under green willows
A fairy whose song
Like the smallest of bubbles
Floats bobbing along;
    Singing down-adown-derry.

Down-adown-derry,
Her cheeks were like wine,
Her eyes in her wee face
Like water-sparks shine,
Her niminy fingers
Her sleek tresses preen,
The which in the combing
She peeps out between;
    Singing down-adown-derry.

Down-adown-derry,
Shrill, shrill was her tune:—
"Come to my water-house,
Annie Maroon:
Come in your dimity,
Ribbon on head,
To wear siller seaweed
And coral instead";
    Singing down-adown-derry.

"Down-adown-derry,
Lean fish of the sea,
Bring lanthorns for feasting
The gay Faërie;
'Tis sand for the dancing,
A music all sweet
In the water-green gloaming
For thistledown feet";
    Singing down-adown-derry.

Down-adown-derry,
Sweet Annie Maroon
Looked large on the fairy
Curled wan as the moon
And all the grey ripples
To the Mill racing by,
With harps and with timbrels
Did ringing reply;
    Singing down-adown-derry.

"Down-adown-derry,"
Sang the Fairy of Doone,
Piercing the heart
Of Sweet Annie Maroon;
And lo! when like roses
The clouds of the sun
Faded at dusk, gone
Was Annie Maroon;
    Singing down-adown-derry.

Down-adown-derry,
The daisies are few;
Frost twinkles powdery
In haunts of the dew;
And only the robin
Perched on a thorn,
Can comfort the heart
Of a father forlorn;
    Singing down-adown-derry.

Down-adown-derry,
There's snow in the air;
Ice where the lily
Bloomed waxen and fair;
He may call o'er the water,
Cry—cry through the Mill,
But Annie Maroon, alas!
Answer ne'er will;
    Singing down-adown-derry.

## THE ENGLISHMAN

I met a sailor in the woods,
    A silver ring wore he,
His hair hung black, his eyes shone blue,
    And thus he said to me:—

'What country, say, of this round earth,
    What shore of what salt sea,
Be this, my son, I wander in,
    And looks so strange to me?'

Says I, 'O foreign sailorman,
    In England now you be,
This is her wood, and this her sky,
    And that her roaring sea.'

He lifts his voice yet louder,
    'What smell be this,' says he,
'My nose on the sharp morning air
    Snuffs up so greedily?'

Says I, 'It is wild roses
    Do smell so winsomely,
And winy briar too,' says I,
    'That in these thickets be.'

'And oh!' says he, 'what leetle bird
    Is singing in yon high tree,
So every shrill and long-drawn note
    Like bubbles breaks in me?'

Says I, 'It is the mavis
    That perches in the tree,
And sings so shrill, and sings so sweet,
    When dawn comes up the sea.'

At which he fell a-musing,
    And fixed his eye on me,
As one alone 'twixt light and dark
    A spirit thinks to see

'England!' he whispers soft and harsh,
    'England!' repeated he,
'And briar, and rose, and mavis,
    A-singing in yon high tree.

'Ye speak me true, my leetle son,
    So—so, it came to me,
A-drifting landwards on a spar,
    And grey dawn on the sea.

'Ay, ay, I could not be mistook;
    I knew them leafy trees,
I knew that land so witcherie sweet,
    And that old noise of seas.

'Though here I've sailed a score of years,
    And heard 'em, dream or wake,
Lap small and hollow 'gainst my cheek,
    On sand and coral break;

'"Yet now, my leetle son," says I,
    A-drifting on the wave,
"That land I see so safe and green
    Is England, I believe.

'"And that there wood is English wood,
    And this here cruel sea,
The selfsame old blue ocean
    Years gone remembers me,

"A-sitting with my bread and butter
    Down ahind yon chitterin' mill;
And this same Marinere"—(that's me),
    "Is that same leetle Will!—

"That very same wee leetle Will
    Eating his bread and butter there,
A-looking on the broad blue sea
    Betwixt his yaller hair!"

'And here be I, my son, throwed up
    Like corpses from the sea,
Ships, stars, winds, tempests, pirates past,
    Yet leetle Will I be!'

He said no more, that sailorman,
    But in a reverie
Stared like the figure of a ship
With painted eyes to sea.

## THE PHANTOM

Upstairs in the large closet, child,
    This side the blue-room door,
Is an old Bible, bound in leather,
    Standing upon the floor;

'Go with this taper, bring it me;
    Carry it on your arm;
It is the book on many a sea
    Hath stilled the waves' alarm.'

Late the hour, dark the night,
    The house is solitary,
Feeble is a taper's light
    To light poor Ann to see.

Her eyes are yet with visions bright
    Of sylph and river, flower and fay,
Now through a narrow corridor
    She takes her lonely way.

Vast shadows on the heedless walls
    Gigantic loom, stoop low:
Each little hasty footfall calls
    Hollowly to and fro.

In the dim solitude her heart
    Remembers tearlessly
White winters when her mother was
    Her loving company.

Now in the dark clear glass she sees
    A taper mocking hers,—
A phantom face of light blue eyes,
    Reflecting phantom fears.

Around her loom the vacant rooms,
    Wind the upward stairs,
She climbs on into a loneliness
    Only her taper shares.

Her grandmother is deaf with age;
    A garden of moonless trees
Would answer not though she should cry
    In anguish on her knees.

So that she scarcely heeds—so fast
    Her pent-up heart doth beat—
When, faint along the corridor,
    Falleth the sound of feet:—

Sounds lighter than silk slippers make
    Upon a ballroom floor, when sweet
Violin and 'cello wake
    Music for twirling feet.

O! in an old unfriendly house,
    What shapes may not conceal
Their faces in the open day,
    At night abroad to steal?

Even her taper seems with fear
    To languish small and blue;
Far in the woods the winter wind
    Runs whistling through.

A dreadful cold plucks at each hair,
    Her mouth is stretched to cry,
But sudden, with a gush of joy,
    It narrows to a sigh.

It is a wilding child which comes
    Swift through the corridor,
Singing an old forgotten song,
    This ancient burden bore:—

'Thorn, thorn, I wis,
And roses twain,
    A red rose and a white,
Stoop in the blossom, bee, and kiss
    A lonely child good-night.

'Swim fish, sing bird,
And sigh again,
   I that am lost am lone,
Bee in the blossom never stirred
   Locks hid beneath a stone!'—

Her eye was of the azure fire
   That hovers in wintry flame;
Her raiment wild and yellow as furze
   That spouteth out the same;

And in her hand she bore no flower,
   But on her head a wreath
Of faded flag-flowers that did yet
   Smell sweetly after death.

Clear was the light of loveliness
   That lit her face like rain;
And sad the mouth that uttered
   Her immemorial strain.

Gloomy with night the corridor
   Is now that she is gone,
Albeit this solitary child
   No longer seems alone.

Fast though her taper dwindles down,
    Heavy and thick the tome,
A beauty beyond fear to dim
    Haunts now her alien home.

Ghosts in the world malignant, grim,
    Vex many a wood, and glen,
And house, and pool,—the unquiet ghosts
    Of dead and restless men.

But in her grannie's house this spirit—
    A child as lone as she—
Pining for love not found on earth,
    Ann dreams again to see.

Seated upon her tapestry-stool,
    Her fairy-book laid by,
She gazes in the fire, knowing
    She hath sweet company.

## HAUNTED

From out the wood I watched them shine,—
    The windows of the haunted house,
Now ruddy as enchanted wine,
    Now dim as flittermouse.

There went a thin voice piping airs
    Along the grey and crooked walks,—
A garden of thistledown and tares,
    Bright leaves, and giant stalks.

The twilight rain shone at its gates,
    Where long-leaved grass in shadow grew;
And black in silence to her mates
    A voiceless raven flew.

Lichen and moss the lone stones greened,
    Green paths led lightly to its door,
Keen from her lair the spider leaned,
    And dusk to darkness wore.

Amidst the sedge a whisper ran,
    The West shut down a heavy eye,
And like last tapers, few and wan,
    The watch-stars kindled in the sky.

## THE SLEEPING BEAUTY

The scent of bramble sweets the air,
    Amid her folded sheets she lies,
The gold of evening in her hair,
    The blue of morn shut in her eyes.

How many a changing moon hath lit
    The unchanging roses of her face!
Her mirror ever broods on it
    In silver stillness of the days.

Oft flits the moth on filmy wings
    Into his solitary lair;
Shrill evensong the cricket sings
    From some still shadow in her hair.

In heat, in snow, in wind, in flood,
    She sleeps in lovely loneliness,
Half folded like an April bud
    On winter-haunted trees.

## THE SUPPER

A wolf he pricks with eyes of fire
Across the night's o'ercrusted snows,
    Seeking his prey,
    He pads his way
Where Jane benighted goes,
    Where Jane benighted goes.

He curdles the bleak air with ire,
Ruffling his hoary raiment through,
    And lo! he sees
    Beneath the trees
Where Jane's light footsteps go,
    Where Jane's light footsteps go.

No hound peals thus in wicked joy,
He snaps his muzzle in the snows,
    His five-clawed feet
    Do scamper fleet
Where Jane's bright lanthorn shows,
    Where Jane's bright lanthorn shows.

Now his greed's green doth gaze unseen
On a pure face of wilding rose,
    Her amber eyes
    In fear's surprise
Watch largely as she goes,
    Watch largely as she goes.

Salt wells his hunger in his jaws,
His lust it revels to and fro,
    Yet small beneath
    A soft voice saith,
'Jane shall in safety go,
    Jane shall in safety go.'

He lurched as if a fiery lash
Had scourged his hide, and through and through,
    His furious eyes
    O'erscanned the skies,
But nearer dared not go,
    But nearer dared not go.

He reared like wild Bucephalus,
His fangs like spears in him uprose,
    Ev'n to the town
    Jane's flitting gown
He grins on as she goes,
    He grins on as she goes.

In fierce lament he howls amain,
He scampers, marvelling in his throes
    What brought him there
    To sup on air,
While Jane unarmèd goes,
    While Jane unarmèd goes.

# THE HORN

Hark! is that a horn I hear,
    In cloudland winding sweet—
And bell-like clash of bridle-rein,
    And silver-shod light feet?

Is it the elfin laughter of
    Fairies riding faint and high,
'Neath the branches of the moon,
    Straying through the starry sky?

Is it in the globèd dew
    Such sweet melodies may fall?
Wood and valley—all are still,
    Hushed the shepherd's call.

Hark! is that a horn I hear
    In cloudland winding sweet?
Or gloomy goblins marching out
    Their captain Puck to greet?

## CAPTAIN LEAN

Out of the East a hurricane
    Swept down on Captain Lean—
That mariner and gentleman
    Will ne'er again be seen.

He sailed his ship against the foes
    Of his own country dear,
But now in the trough of the billows
    An aimless course doth steer.

Powder was violets to his nostril,
    Sweet the din of the fighting-line,
Now he is flotsam on the seas,
    And his bones are bleached with brine.

The stars move up along the sky,
    The moon she shines so bright,
And in that solitude the foam
    Sparkles unearthly white.

This is the tomb of Captain Lean,
    Would a straiter please his soul?
I trow he sleeps in peace,
    Howsoever the billows roll!

# THE PORTRAIT OF A WARRIOR

His brow is seamed with line and scar;
    His cheek is red and dark as wine;
The fires as of a Northern star
    Beneath his cap of sable shine.

His right hand, bared of leathern glove,
    Hangs open like an iron gin,
You stoop to see his pulses move,
    To hear the blood sweep out and in.

He looks some king, so solitary
    In earnest thought he seems to stand,
As if across a lonely sea
    He gazed impatient of the land.

Out of the noisy centuries
    The foolish and the fearful fade;
Yet burn unquenched these warrior eyes,
    Time hath not dimmed nor death dismayed.

## THE ISLE OF LONE

Three dwarfs there were which lived on an isle,
    And the name of the isle was Lone,
And the names of the dwarfs were Alliolyle,
    Lallerie, Muziomone.

Their house was small and sweet of the sea,
    And pale as the Malmsey wine;
Their bowls were three, and their beds were three,
    And their nightcaps white were nine.

Their beds were of the holly-wood,
    Their combs of the tortoiseshell,
Their mirrors clear as wintry flood,
    Frozen dark and snell.

Green rushes, green rushes lay thick on the floor,
    For light beamed a goblet of wax;
There were three wooden stools for whatever they wore
    On their humpity-dumpity backs.

So each would lie on his plumpy pillow,
    And watch the moon in the sky—
And hear the parrot scream to the billow,
    And the billow roar reply:

Parrots of sapphire and sulphur and amber,
    Amethyst, azure and green,
While apes in the plain trees did scramble and clamber
    Hairy and hungry and lean.

All night long with bubbles a-glisten
    The ocean cried under the moon,
Till ape and parrot too sleepy to listen
    To sleep and slumber were gone.

Then from three small beds the dark hours' while
    In a house in the Island of Lone
Rose the snoring of Lallerie, Alliolyle,
    The snoring of Muziomone.

But soon as ever came peep of sun
On coral and feathery tree,
Three night-capped dwarfs to the surf would run
And soon were a-bob in the sea.

At six they went fishing, at nine to snare
    Young foxes in the dells,
At noon in the shade on sweet fruits did fare,
    And blew in their twisted shells.

Dark was the sea they gambolled in,
    And thick with silver fish,
Dark as green glass blown clear and thin
    To be a monarch's dish.

They sate to sup in a jasmine bower,
    Lit pale with flies of fire,
Their bowls the hue of the iris-flower,
    And lemon their attire.

Sweet wine in little cups they sipped,
    And golden honeycomb
Into their bowls of cream they dipped,
    Whipt light and white as foam.

Now Alliolyle, where the sand-flower blows
    Taught three old apes to sing—
Taught three old apes to dance on their toes
    And caper around in a ring.

They yelled the hoarse and they croaked them sweet,
    They twirled them about and around,
To the noise of their voices they danced with their feet,
    They stamped with their feet on the ground.

But down to the shore skipped Lallerie,
    His parrot on his thumb,
And the twain they scritched in mockery,
    While the dancers go and come.

So, alas! in the evening, rosy and still,
    Light-haired Lallerie
Bitterly quarrelled with Alliolyle
    By the yellow-sanded sea.

The rising moon swam sweet and large
    Before their furious eyes,
And they rolled and rolled to the coral marge
    Where the surf for ever cries.

Too late, too late, comes Muziomone:
    Clear in the clear green sea
Alliolyle lies not alone,
    But clasped with Lallerie.

He blows on his shell plaintive notes;
    Ape, parraquito, bee
Flock where a shoe on the salt wave floats,—
    The shoe of Lallerie.

He fetches nightcaps, one and nine,
    Grey apes he dowers three,
His house as fair as the Malmsey wine
    Seems sad as cypress-tree.

Three bowls he brims with honeycomb
    To feast the bumble bees,
Saying, 'O bees, be this your home,
    For grief is on the seas!'

He sate him lone in a coral grot,
    At the flowing of the tide;
When ebbed the billow, there was not,
    Save coral, aught beside.

So hairy apes in three white beds,
    And nightcaps, one and nine,
On moonlit pillows lay three heads
    Bemused with dwarfish wine.

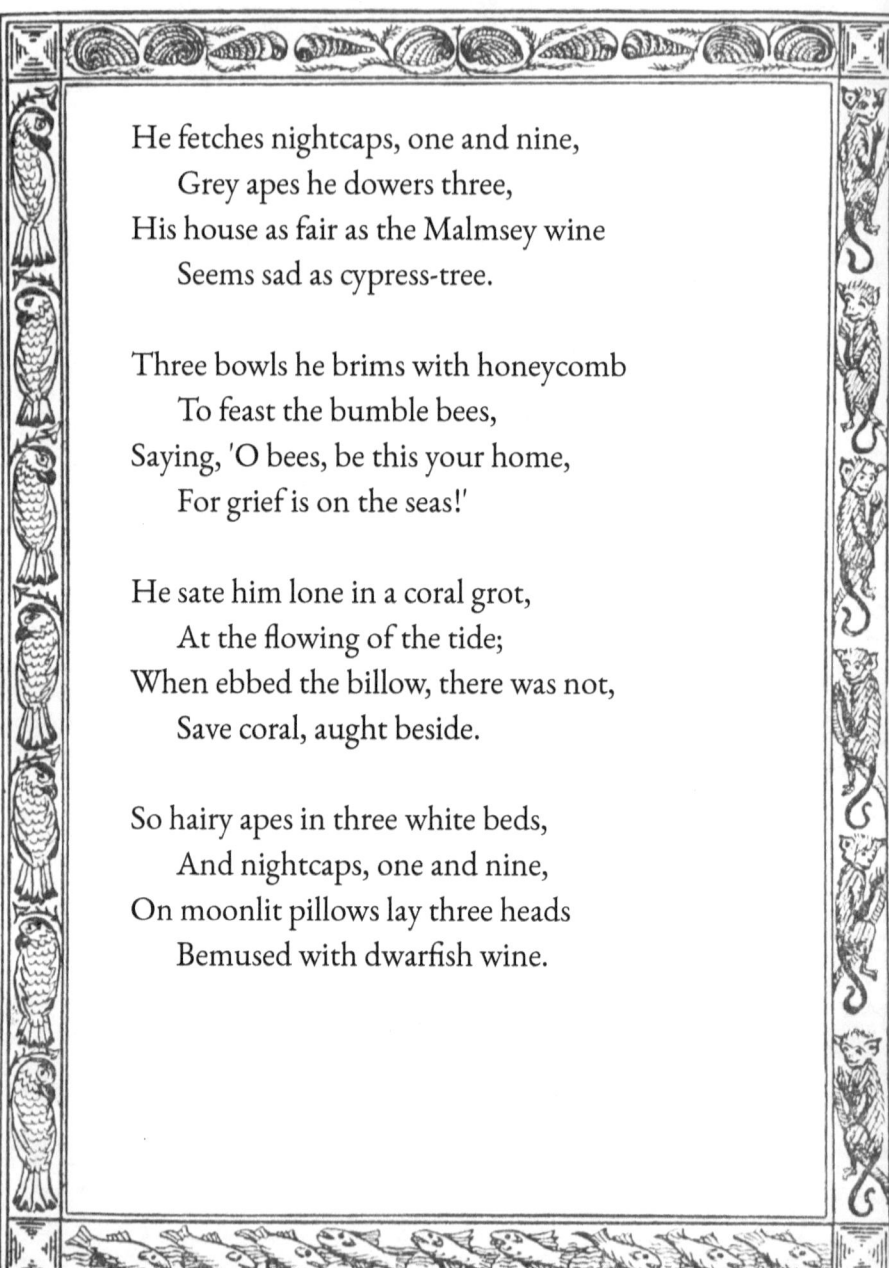

A tomb of coral, the dirge of bee,
    The grey apes' guttural groan
For Alliolyle, for Lallerie,
    For thee, O Muziomone!

## THE RAVEN'S TOMB

'Build me my tomb,' the Raven said,
'Within the dark yew-tree,
So in the Autumn yewberries
Sad lamps may burn for me.
Summon the haunted beetle,
From twilight bud and bloom,
To drone a gloomy dirge for me
At dusk above my tomb.
Beseech ye too the glowworm
To bear her cloudy flame,
Where the small, flickering bats resort,
Whistling in tears my name.
Let the round dew a whisper make,
Welling on twig and thorn;
And only the grey cock at night
Call through his silver horn.
And you, dear sisters, don your black
For ever and a day,
To show how sweet a raven
In his tomb is laid away.'

# THE CHRISTENING

The bells chime clear,
   Soon will the sun behind the hills
       sink down;
Come, little Ann, your baby brother
       dear
Lies in his christening-gown.

His godparents
Are all across the fields stepped on before,
And wait beneath the crumbling monuments,
This side the old church door.

Your mammie dear
Leans frail and lovely on your daddie's arm;
Watching her chick, 'twixt happiness and fear,
Lest he should come to harm.

All to be blest
Full soon in the clear heavenly water, he
Sleeps on unwitting of't, his little breast
Heaving so tenderly.

I carried you,
My little Ann, long since on this same quest,
And from the painted windows a pale hue
Lit golden on your breast;

And then you woke,
Chill as the holy water trickled down,
And, weeping, cast the window a strange look,
Half smile, half infant frown.

I scarce could hear
The larks a-singing in the green meadows,
'Twas summertide, and budding far and near
The hedges thick with rose.

And now you're grown
A little girl, and this same helpless mite
Is come like such another bud half-blown,
Out of the wintry night.

Time flies, time flies!
And yet, bless me! 'tis little changed am I;
May Jesu keep from tears those infant eyes,
Be love their lullaby!

# THE FUNERAL

They dressed us up in black,
 Susan and Tom and me;
And, walking through the fields
All beautiful to see,
With brances high in the hair
And daisy and buttercup,
We heard the lark in the clouds--
In black dressed up.

The took us to the graves,
Susan and Tom and me,
Where the long grasses grow
And the funeral tree:
We stood and watched; and the wind
Came softly out of the sky
And blew in Susan's hair,
As I stood close by.

Back through the fields we came,
Tom and Susan and me,
And we sat in the nursery together,
And had our tea.
And, looking out of the window,
I heard the thrushes sing;
But Tom fell asleep in his chair.
He was so tired, poor thing.

## THE MOTHER BIRD

Through the green twilight of a hedge
I peered, with cheek on the cool leaves pressed,
And spied a bird upon a nest:
Two eyes she had beseeching me
Meekly and brave, and her brown breast
Throbb'd hot and quick above her heart;
And then she oped her dagger bill,—
'Twas not a chirp, as sparrows pipe
At break of day; 'twas not a trill,
As falters through the quiet even;
But one sharp solitary note,
One desperate, fierce, and vivid cry
Of valiant tears, and hopeless joy,
One passionate note of victory:
Off, like a fool afraid, I sneaked,
Smiling the smile the fool smiles best,
At the mother bird in the secret hedge
Patient upon her lonely nest.

## THE CHILD IN THE STORY GOES TO BED

I prythee, Nurse, come smooth my hair,
   And prythee, Nurse, unloose my shoe,
And trimly turn my silken sheet
    Upon my quilt of gentle blue.

My pillow sweet of lavender
    Smooth with an amiable hand,
And may the dark pass peacefully by
    As in the hour-glass droops the sand.

Prepare my cornered manchet sweet,
    And in my little crystal cup
Pour out the blithe and flowering mead
    That forthwith I may sup.

Withdraw my curtains from the night,
    And let the crispèd crescent shine
Upon my eyelids while I sleep,
    And soothe me with her beams benign.

From far-away there streams the singing
    Of the mellifluent nightingale,—
Surely if goblins hear her lay,
    They shall not o'er my peace prevail.

Now quench my silver lamp, prythee,
    And bid the harpers harp that tune
Fairies which haunt the meadowlands
    Sing clearly to the stars of June.

And bid them play, though I in dreams
    No longer heed their pining strains,
For I would not to silence wake
    When slumber o'er my senses wanes.

You Angels bright who me defend,
    Enshadow me with curvèd wing,
And keep me in the darksome night
    Till dawn another day do bring.

## THE CHILD IN THE STORY AWAKES

The light of dawn rose on my dreams,
    And from afar I seemed to hear
In sleep the mellow blackbird call
    Hollow and sweet and clear.

I prythee, Nurse, my casement open,
    Wildly the garden peals with singing,
And hooting through the dewy pines
    The goblins all are winging.

O listen the droning of the bees,
    That in the roses take delight!
And see a cloud stays in the blue
    Like an angel still and bright.

The gentle sky is spread like silk,
    And, Nurse, the moon doth languish there,
As if it were a perfect jewel
    In the morning's soft-spun hair.

The greyness of the distant hills
    Is silvered in the lucid East,
See, now the sheeny-plumèd cock
    Wags haughtily his crest.

'O come you out, O come you out,
    Lily, and lavender, and lime;
The kingcup swings his golden bell,
    And plumpy cherries drum the time.

'O come you out, O come you out!
    Roses, and dew, and mignonette,
The sun is in the steep blue sky,
    Sweetly the morning star is set.'

## CECIL

Ye little elves, who haunt sweet dells,
    Where flowers with the dew commune,
I pray you hush the child, Cecil,
    With windlike song.

O little elves, so white she lieth,
Each eyelid gentler than the flow'r
Of the bramble, and her fleecy hair
    Like smoke of gold.

O little elves, her hands and feet
The angels muse upon, and God
Hath shut a glimpse of Paradise
    In each blue eye.

O little elves, her tiny body
Like a white flake of snow it is,
Drooping upon the pale green hood
    Of the chill snowdrop.

O little elves, with elderflower,
And pimpernel, and the white hawthorn,
Sprinkle the journey of her dreams:
    And, little elves,

Call to her magically sweet,
Lest of her very tenderness
She do forsake this rough brown earth
    And return to us no more.

# THE LAMPLIGHTER

When the light of day declines,
And a swift angel through the sky
Kindles God's tapers clear,
With ashen staff the lamplighter
Passes along the darkling streets
To light our earthly lamps;

Lest, prowling in the darkness,
The thief should haunt with quiet tread,
Or men on evil errands set;
Or wayfarers be benighted;
Or neighbours bent from house to house
Should need a guiding torch.

He is like a needlewoman
Who deftly on a sable hem
Stitches in gleaming jewels;
Or, haply, he is like a hero,
Whose bright deeds on the long journey
Are beacons on our way.

And when in the East comes morning,
And the broad splendour of the sun,
Then, with the tune of little birds
Ringing on high, the lamplighter
Passes by each quiet house,
And he puts out the lamps.

## I MET AT EVE

I met at eve the Prince of Sleep,
His was a still and lovely face,
He wandered through a valley steep
    Lovely in a lonely place.

His garb was grey of lavender,
About his brows a poppy-wreath
Burned like dim coals, and everywhere
    The air was sweeter for his breath.

His twilight feet no sandals wore,
His eyes shone faint in their own flame,
Fair moths that gloomed his steps before
    Seemed letters of his lovely name.

His house is in the mountain ways,
A phantom house of misty walls,
Whose golden flocks at evening graze,
    And witch the moon with muffled calls.

Upwelling from his shadowy springs
Sweet waters shake a trembling sound,
There flit the hoot-owl's silent wings,
    There hath his web the silkworm wound.

Dark in his pools clear visions lurk,
And rosy, as with morning buds,
Along his dales of broom and birk
    Dreams haunt his solitary woods.

I met at eve the Prince of Sleep,
His was a still and lovely face,
He wandered through a valley steep,
    Lovely in a lonely place.

## LULLABY

Sleep, sleep, lovely white soul!
The singing mouse sings plaintively,
The sweet night-bird in the chesnut-tree—
They sing together, bird and mouse,
In starlight, in darkness, lonely, sweet,
The wild notes and the faint notes meet—
    Sleep, sleep, lovely white soul!

Sleep, sleep, lovely white soul!
Amid the lilies floats the moth,
The mole along his galleries goeth
In the dark earth; the summer moon
Looks like a shepherd through the pane
Seeking his feeble lamb again—
    Sleep, sleep, lovely white soul!

Sleep, sleep, lovely white soul!
Time comes to keep night-watch with thee
Nodding with roses; and the sea
Saith 'Peace! Peace!' amid his foam
White as thy night-clothes; 'O be still!'
The wind cries up the whisp'ring hill—
    Sleep, sleep, lovely white soul!

## ENVOY

Child, do you love the flower
Ashine with colour and dew
Lighting its transient hour?
    So I love you.

The lambs in the mead are at play,
'Neath a hurdle the shepherd's asleep,
From height to height of the day
    The sunbeams sweep.

Evening will come. And alone
The dreamer the dark will beguile;
All the world will be gone
    For a dream's brief while.

Then I shalle be old; and away;
And you, with sad joy in your eyes,
Will brood over children at play
    With as loveful surmise.

## THE HORSEMAN

I heard a horseman
    Ride over the hill;
The moon shone clear,
    The night was still;
His helm was silver,
    And pale was he;
And the horse he rode
    Was of ivory.

## UP AND DOWN

Down the Hill of Ludgate,
    Up the Hill of Fleet,
To and fro and East and West
    With people flows the street;
Even the King of England
    On Temple Bar must beat
For leave to ride to Ludgate
    Down the Hill of Fleet.

## MRS. EARTH

Mrs. Earth makes silver black,
    Mrs. Earth makes iron red
But Mrs. Earth can not stain gold,
    Nor ruby red.
Mrs. earth the slenderest bone
    Whitens in her bosom cold,
But Mrs. Earth can change my dreams
    No more than ruby or gold.
Mrs. Earth and Mr. Sun
    Can tan my skin, and tire my toes,
But all that I'm thinking of, ever shall think,
    Why, either knows.

## ALAS, ALACK!

Ann, Ann!
    Come! Quick as you can!
There's a fish that talks
    In the frying-pan.
Out of the fat,
    As clear as glass,
He put up his mouth
    And moaned 'Alas!'
Oh, most mournful,
    'Alas, alack!'
Then turned to his sizzling,
    And sank him back.

WALTER DE LA MARE
# TIRED TIM

Poor Tired Tim! It's sad for him.
    He lags the long bright morning through,
Ever so tired of nothing to do;
    He moons and mopes the livelong day,
Nothing to think about, nothing to say;
    Up to bed with his candle to creep,
Too tired to yawn, too tired to sleep:
    Poor Tired Tim! It's sad for him.


# MIMA

Jemima is my name,
    But oh, I have another;
My father always calls me Meg,
    And so do Bob and mother;
Only my sister, jealous of
    The strands of my bright hair,
'Jemima – Mima – Mima!'
    Calls, mocking, up the stair.

## THE HUNTSMEN

Three jolly gentlemen,
   In coats of red,
Rode their horses
   Up to bed.
Three jolly gentlemen
   Snored till morn,
Their horses champing
   The golden corn.
Three jolly gentlemen,
   At break of day,
Came clitter-clatter down the stairs
   And galloped away.

## THE BANDOG

Has anybody seen my Mopser? —
   A comely dog is he,
With hair of the colour of a Charles the Fifth,
   And teeth like ships at sea,
His tail it curls straight upwards,
   His ears stand two abreast,
And he answers to the simple name of Mopser
   When civilly addressed.

# I CAN'T ABEAR

I can't abear a Butcher,
    I can't abide his meat,
The ugliest shop of all is his,
    The ugliest in the street;
Bakers' are warm, cobblers' dark,
    Chemists' burn watery lights;
But oh, the sawdust butcher's shop,
    That ugliest of sights!

# THE DUNCE

Why does he still keep ticking?
    Why does his round white face
Stare at me over the books and ink,
    And mock at my disgrace?
Why does that thrush call, 'Dunce, dunce, dunce!'?
    Why does that bluebottle buzz?
Why does the sun so silent shine? —
    And what do I care if it does?

## CHICKEN

Clapping her platter stood plump Bess,
    And all across the green
Came scampering in, on wing and claw,
    Chicken fat and lean:
Dorking, Spaniard, Cochin China,
    Bantams sleek and small,
Like feathers blown in a great wind,
    They came at Bessie's call.

## SOME ONE

Some one came knocking
    At my wee, small door;
Some one came knocking,
    I'm sure – sure – sure;
I listened, I opened,
    I looked to left and right,
But naught there was a-stirring
    In the still dark night;
Only the busy beetle
    Tap-tapping in the wall,
Only from the forest
    The screech-owl's call,
Only the cricket whistling
    While the dewdrops fall,
So I know not who came knocking,
    At all, at all, at all.

# BREAD AND CHERRIES

'Cherries, ripe cherries!'
   The old woman cried,
In her snowy white apron,
   And basket beside;
And the little boys came,
   Eyes shining, cheeks red,
To buy a bag of cherries,
   To eat with their bread.

# OLD SHELLOVER

'Come!' said Old Shellover.
'What?' says Creep.
'The horny old Gardener's fast asleep;
The fat cock Thrush
To his nest has gone;
And the dew shines bright
In the rising Moon;
Old Sallie Worm from her hole doth peep:
Come!' said Old Shellover.
'Aye!' said Creep.

## HAPLESS

Hapless, hapless, I must be
   All the hours of life I see,
Since my foolish nurse did once
   Bed me on her leggen bones;
Since my mother did not weel
   To snip my nails with blades of steel.
Had they laid me on a pillow
   In a cot of water willow,
Had they bitten finger and thumb,
   Not to such ill hap I had come.

## THE LITTLE BIRD

My dear Daddie bought a mansion
   For to bring my Mammie to,
In a hat with a long feather,
   And a trailing gown of blue;
And a company of fiddlers
   And a rout of maids and men
Danced the clock round to the morning,
   In a gay house-warming then.
And when all the guests were gone, and
   All was still as still can be,
In from the dark ivy hopped a
   Wee small bird: and that was Me.

## CAKE AND SACK

Old King Caraway
    Supped on cake,
And a cup of sack
    His thirst to slake;
Bird in arras
    And hound in hall
Watched very softly
    Or not at all;
Fire in the middle,
    Stone all round
Changed not, heeded not,
    Made no sound;
All by himself
    At the Table High
He'd nibble and sip
    While his dreams slipped by;
And when he had finished,
    He'd nod and say,
'Cake and sack
    For King Caraway!'

# THE SHIP OF RIO

There was a ship of Rio
    Sailed out into the blue,
And nine and ninety monkeys
    Were all her jovial crew.
From bo'sun to the cabin boy,
    From quarter to caboose,
There weren't a stitch of calico
    To breech 'em – tight or loose;
From spar to deck, from deck to keel,
    From barnacle to shroud,
There weren't one pair of reach-me-downs
    To all that jabbering crowd.
But wasn't it a gladsome sight,
    When roared the deep sea gales,
To see them reef her fore and aft
    A-swinging by their tails!
Oh, wasn't it a gladsome sight,
    When glassy calm did come,
To see them squatting tailor-wise
    Around a keg of rum!
Oh, wasn't it a gladsome sight,
    When in she sailed to land,
To see them all a-scampering skip
    For nuts across the sand!

# TILLIE

Old Tillie Turveycombe
Sat to sew,
Just where a patch of fern did grow;
There, as she yawned,
And yawn wide did she,
Floated some seed
Down her gull-e-t;
And look you once,
And look you twice,
Poor old Tillie
Was gone in a trice.
But oh, when the wind
Do a-moaning come,
'Tis poor old Tillie
Sick for home;
And oh, when a voice
In the mist do sigh,
Old Tillie Turveycombe's
Floating by.

## JIM JAY

Do diddle di do,
    Poor Jim Jay
Got stuck fast
    In Yesterday.
Squinting he was,
    On Cross-legs bent,
Never heeding
    The wind was spent.
Round veered the weathercock,
    The sun drew in -
And stuck was Jim
    Like a rusty pin...
We pulled and we pulled
    From seven till twelve,
Jim, too frightened
    To help himself.
But all in vain.
    The clock struck one,
And there was Jim
    A little bit gone.
At half-past five
    You scarce could see
A glimpse of his flapping
    Handkerchee.

And when came noon,
    And we climbed sky-high,
Jim was a speck
    Slip – slipping by.
Come to-morrow,
    The neighbours say,
He'll be past crying for;
    Poor Jim Jay.

## MISS T.

It's a very odd thing —
    As odd as can be —
That whatever Miss T. eats
    Turns into Miss T.;
Porridge and apples,
    Mince, muffins and mutton,
Jam, junket, jumbles —
    Not a rap, not a button
It matters; the moment
    They're out of her plate,
Though shared by Miss Butcher
    And sour Mr. Bate;
Tiny and cheerful,
    And neat as can be,
Whatever Miss T. eats
    Turns into Miss T.

## THE CUPBOARD

I know a little cupboard,
With a teeny tiny key,
And there's a jar of Lollypops
    For me, me, me.

It has a little shelf, my dear,
As dark as dark can be,
And there's a dish of Banbury Cakes
    For me, me, me.

I have a small fat grandmamma,
With a very slippery knee,
And she's the Keeper of the Cupboard
    With the key, key, key.

And I'm very good, my dear,
As good as good can be,
There's Branbury Cakes, and Lollypops
    For me, me, me.

## THE BARBER'S

Gold locks, and black locks,
    Red locks and brown,
Topknot to love-curl
    The hair wisps down;
Straight above the clear eyes,
    Rounded round the ears,
Snip-snap and snick-a-snick,
    Clash the Barber's shears;
Us, in the looking-glass,
    Footsteps in the street,
Over, under, to and fro,
    The lean blades meet;
Bay Rum or Bear's Grease,
    A silver groat to pay -
Then out a-shin-shan-shining
    In the bright, blue day.

## HIDE AND SEEK

Hide and seek, says the Wind,
    In the shade of the woods;
Hide and seek, says the Moon,
    To the hazel buds;
Hide and seek, says the Cloud,
    Star on to star;
Hide and seek, says the Wave,
    At the harbour bar;
Hide and seek, say I,
    To myself, and step
Out of the dream of Wake
    Into the dream of Sleep.

## BOYS AND GIRLS

## THEN

Twenty, forty, sixty, eighty
    A hundred years ago,
All through the night with lantern bright
      The Watch trudged to and fro,
And little boys tucked snug abed
    Would wake from dreams to hear -
'Two o' the morning by the clock,
    And the stars a-shining clear!'
Or, when across the chimney-tops
    Screamed shrill a North-East gale,
A faint and shaken voice would shout,
    'Three! And a storm of hail!'


## THE WINDOW

Behind the blinds I sit and watch
The people passing – passing by;
And not a single one can see
    My tiny watching eye.

They cannot see my little room,
All yellowed with the shaded sun;
They do not even know I'm here;
    Nor'll guess when I am gone.

## POOR HENRY

Thick in its glass
   The physic stands,
Poor Henry lifts
   Distracted hands;
His round cheek wans
   In the candlelight,
To smell that smell!
   To see that sight!

Finger and thumb
   Clinch his small nose,
A gurgle, a gasp,
   And down it goes;
Scowls Henry now;
   But mark that cheek,
Sleek with the bloom
   Of health next week!

## FULL MOON

One night as Dick lay half asleep,
   Into his drowsy eyes
A great still light begins to creep
   From out the silent skies.
It was lovely moon's, for when
   He raised his dreamy head,
Her surge of silver filled the pane
   And streamed across his bed.
So, for a while, each gazed at each -
   Dick and the solemn moon -
Till, climbing slowly on her way,
   She vanished, and was gone.

## THE BOOKWORM

'I'm tired – Oh, tired of books,' said Jack,
    'I long for meadows green,
And woods, where shadowy violets
    Nod their cool leaves between;
I long to see the ploughman stride
    His darkening acres o'er,
To hear the hoarse sea-waters drive
    Their billows 'gainst the shore;
I long to watch the sea-mew wheel
    Back to her rock-perched mate;
Or, where the breathing cows are housed,
    Lean dreaming o'er the gate.
Something has gone, and ink and print
    Will never bring it back;
I long for the green fields again,
    I'm tired of books,' said Jack.

# THE QUARTETTE

Tom sang for joy and Ned sang for joy and old
    Sam sang for joy;
All we four boys piped up loud, just like one boy;
And the ladies that sate with the Squire – their
    cheeks were all wet,
For the noise of the voice of us boys, when we
    sang our Quartette.

Tom he piped low and Ned he piped low and old
    Sam he piped low;
Into a sorrowful fall did our music flow;
And the ladies that sate with the Squire vowed
    they'd never forget
How the eyes of them cried for delight, when we
    sang our Quartette.

# MISTLETOE

Sitting under the mistletoe
(Pale-green, fairy mistletoe),
One last candle burning low,
All the sleepy dancers gone,
Just one candle burning on,
Shadows lurking everywhere:
Some one came, and kissed me there.

Tired I was; my head would go
Nodding under the mistletoe
(Pale-green, fairy mistletoe),
No footsteps came, no voice, but only,
Just as I sat there, sleepy, lonely,
Stooped in the still and shadowy air
Lips unseen – and kissed me there.

## THE LOST SHOE

Poor little Lucy
   By some mischance,
Lost her shoe
   As she did dance -
'Twas not on the stairs,
   Not in the hall;
Not where they sat
   At supper at all.
She looked in the garden,
   But there it was not;
Henhouse, or kennel,
   Or high dovecote.
Dairy and meadow,
   And wild woods through
Showed not a trace
   Of Lucy's shoe.
Bird nor bunny
   Nor glimmering moon
Breathed a whisper
   Of where 'twas gone.
It was cried and cried,
   Oyez and Oyez!
In French, Dutch, Latin,
   And Portuguese.

Ships the dark seas
   Went plunging through,
But none brought news
   Of Lucy's shoe;
And still she patters
   In silk and leather,
O'er snow, sand, shingle,
   In every weather;
Spain, and Africa,
   Hindustan,
Java, China,
   And lamped Japan;
Plain and desert,
   She hops-hops through,
Pernambuco
   To gold Peru;
Mountain and forest,
   And river too,
All the world over
   For her lost shoe.

## THE TRUANTS

Ere my heart beats too coldly and faintly
    To remember sad things, yet be gay,
I would sing a brief song of the world's little children
    Magic hath stolen away.

The primroses scattered by April,
    The stars of the wide Milky Way,
Cannot outnumber the hosts of the children
    Magic hath stolen away.

The buttercup green of the meadows,
    The snow of the blossoming may,
Lovelier are not than the legions of children
    Magic hath stolen away.

The waves tossing surf in the moonbeam,
    The albatross lone on the spray,
Alone know the tears wept in vain for the children
    Magic hath stolen away.

In vain: for at hush of the evening,
    When the stars twinkle into the grey,
Seems to echo the far-away calling of children
    Magic hath stolen away.

www.ingramcontent.com/pod-product-compliance
Lightning Source LLC
Chambersburg PA
CBHW031119080526
44587CB00011B/1034